Dear Cheryl,
You are precious
to God.
Tracy

The African rand features a wildebeest.

Treasures
of the Wise

TRACY L. SMOAK

Treasures
of the Wise

30 DEVOTIONS FOR
STORING UP HEAVENLY RICHES

Ambassador International
GREENVILLE, SOUTH CAROLINA & BELFAST, NORTHERN IRELAND

www.ambassador-international.com

Magnifying Jesus while promoting His gospel through the written word.

PRAISE FOR
Treasures of the Wise

Tracy has a gift to see God's presence all around us every day. These devotions are filled with insightful observations relevant to everyone. I recommend this guide to discover treasures of wisdom and knowledge in the Bible.

~**Tim Smith**, financial advisor, group facilitator for Dave Ramsey's Financial Peace University

Very nicely done collection of short devotions. Smoak shows us that there are treasures in ordinary things, and she attaches a spiritual lesson to each. The photos are beautiful and add to each entry.

~**Susan Snodgrass,** Christian book reviewer, blogger for *Simply Susan*

Tracy aligns poignant use of Scripture with her own beautiful photography. Steeped in the Christian tradition, Tracy is biblically wise. This book will deeply bless your devotional time.

~**Rev. Beth Knight,** ordained minister with the Federation of Christian Ministries

This well-written book provides guidance on how rewarding it is to have God well within your soul.

~**Robbie Boswell,** information technology program manager, banking industry

The photographs are beautiful, and I love the concept of connecting a coin collection to the Bible's "treasures of wisdom." Readers will be blessed by this book!

~**Rhoda Preston,** retired elder in the Iowa Annual Conference of the United Methodist Church

Much like a daily study of a proverb, this book should be required reading. It has an "everyman" appeal in a timely, real-world setting. I enjoyed it very much.

~**Frank Gammon,** real estate investor

ISBN: 978-1-64960-721-8, Hardcover
ISBN: 978-1-64960-608-2, Paperback
eISBN: 978-1-64960-659-4

AMBASSADOR INTERNATIONAL
Emerald House
411 University Ridge, Suite B14
Greenville, SC. 29601
www.ambassador-international.com

AMBASSADOR INTERNATIONAL BOOKS
The Mount
2 Woodstock Link
Belfast, BT6 8DD, Northern Ireland, UK
www.ambassadormedia.co.uk

The colophon is a trademark of Ambassador, a Christian publishing company.

These foreign coins are part of a collection from travels.
On the left, the Japanese ten-yen features the UNESCO World Heritage site of the
Byodoin Temple, which initially was a palace retreat.
Center, the Italian five-hundred-lire design includes Hermes, herald of the gods and
protector of merchants. The owl on the Greek drachma represents the ability to see truth,
which would be revealed to Athena, the goddess of wisdom.
Money is an important factor of life because coins carry cultural symbols
and connect to the heart of what we value.

Contents

What knowledge unlocks how to live a successful life,
according to God's principles?
Read on for Scriptures to guide daily choices
and gain peace of mind.

Contents

My goal is that they may be encouraged in heart and united in love,

so that they may have the full riches of complete understanding,

in order that they may know the mystery of God, namely, Christ,

in whom are hidden all the treasures of wisdom and knowledge.

Colossians 2:2

Introduction

The phrase, "A penny for your thoughts," is believed to have become popular in the 1500s. Centuries later, the expression still suggests we can reap rewards from our daily reflections. Business writer Zachary Crockett estimates we have about fifty thoughts per minute. According to him, that nets close to $700 daily, with an annual take-home exceeding $255,000.[1] If that much earning potential exists in our intellectual capital, don't we want to invest wisely for good returns?

This devotional features thirty meditations about how to secure a rich spiritual reward. Each devotion to store up heavenly treasures begins with history found on foreign coins. My collection of coins grew during decades of travel to areas such as Africa, Europe, Mongolia, and the Caribbean. In this book, you'll find cultural insights paired with modern photographs, Bible verses, and prayers for keeping centered on what counts most in life. Rather than crunching numbers about gaining financial assets, the spiritual journey maps how to balance the desires of our heart with God's purpose for our lives.

The Bible is a treasure trove of history and advice declaring
God's love for us throughout all generations. The King James Version,
approved in 1611, gave lay people access to the Bible and remains
the most widely published text in the English language.[2]

Treasure One
The Bible Reveals God's Mysteries

Travel broadens our perspectives.
My son brought this 1977 coin back
from the Republic of Djibouti.
I am intrigued by the camels and
the idea of ancient civilizations
connecting to our world today.

Museum exhibits of the Dead Sea Scrolls display ancient slivers of yellowed parchment with slender black lines of script. The relics found in Qumran date back two thousand years to a time when Israel reigned at the crossroads of three continents—Europe, Asia, and Africa. Once secreted in clay jars stored in eleven desert caves, the relics record undeniable history. Whether we read a King James Version—"Thus sayeth the Lord"—or scroll through an electronic tablet for modern translations, God provides the Bible for us to know His heart and study His guidelines. The richness of His Word offers unparalleled instructions on how to invest in heavenly treasures.

⸎

God doesn't come and go. God lasts. He's Creator of all you can see or imagine.

He doesn't get tired out, doesn't pause to catch his breath.

And he knows everything, inside and out.

Isaiah 40:28 MSG

Today's Prayer
Dear Lord, You spoke centuries ago to scribes who faithfully wrote down Your teachings. Please grant us the ability to understand Your Word and apply the lessons to our lives. We seek wisdom to treasure.
Amen.

A heart willing to seek God is golden.
To make stained glass, narrow strips of lead form the pattern
and hold together the pieces of glass.
The lead is flexible and adaptable.
These characteristics work well for an attitude
of following God and allowing Him
to shape us.

Treasure Two
God Favors a Willing Heart

Dated 1973, this fifty-pence piece is from England.
I spent a fall semester there in college.
The image of hands working together reminds me
of the value in sharing whatever gifts we have
with a cheerful heart to help others.
Living overseas, I benefited from the kindness of others.

Light reveals hidden colors in stained-glass artwork, and God shows us what is in our hearts. In places where we are selfish or bitter, He shines awareness so we can change and grow and become more generous. His unconditional love and gentleness guide us to develop talents that serve others rather than ourselves. He crafts our experiences into beautiful masterpieces. When we choose to please Him, we radiate joy.

Take from among you an offering to the LORD. Whoever is of a willing heart, let
him bring it as an offering to the LORD: gold, silver, and bronze; blue, purple, and
scarlet thread, fine linen …
Exodus 35:5-6 NKJV

Today's Prayer
Dear Lord, my focus is often on myself. I forget to look at the mosaic of how You are
working in many lives and how I can contribute resources You have allotted to me.
Please show me how to shimmer with a cheerful heart, eager to do Your will.
Amen.

The black swallowtail caterpillar dines on parsley.
Spending its first week or so as a single egg laid on a host plant,
the larva generally develops in ten to thirty days.[3]
The pupal stage is from nine to eighteen days.

Treasure Three
God Transforms Circumstances

Greeks printed the sphinx on the 1973 drachma.
Caterpillars rise up from the cocoon
as the mythical bird did to see new life.
We do the same with Christ.

At each stage of life, we have different needs and abilities. When we trust God to guide us through every phase, we can be assured there is nothing to fear. We will become the glorious best He intends us to be. From landlocked caterpillars, we can transform into winged butterflies ascending into the skies.

For our citizenship is in heaven, from which
we also eagerly wait for the Savior, the Lord Jesus Christ,
who will transform our lowly body that it may be conformed
to His glorious body, according to the working by which He is able
even to subdue all things to Himself.
Philippians 3:20-21 NKJV

Today's Prayer
Dear Lord, change isn't easy. We get caught up in circumstances and can't see how anything could be better.
We think outcomes are certain, and we settle for far less than the glorious vision you have.
Please teach us contentment in the place where we await your developments.
Amen.

This puppy is a twelve-week-old Labradoodle mix.
He knows how to sit on command and quickly plants his behind to wait
for instruction. His prized possession is the deflated soccer ball he trundles
around the yard. He likes having his owner chase him, innovating
a game of his own, the rules of which his humans have yet to decipher.

Treasure Four
Obedience Nets Opportunity

Eire on this twenty-pence coin
is the Irish Gaelic name for Ireland.[4]
The noble image, dated 1986, reminds me
of the majesty of horses surrendered in obedience to their riders.
The animals are not weak; rather, they are alert to orders.
Our strength is not compromised when we yield to God's direction.
Instead, it is enhanced.

Pets can be delightful. The furry creatures snuggle close and adore us, even when we aren't at our best. They offer companionship. Young ones need time and patient coaching to understand what is expected, and what a joy it is when they cooperate. As they mature, more freedoms are offered with an established routine. The way they express affection is not complicated; they enjoy being by our sides.

Having confidence in your obedience,
I write to you, knowing that you will do even more than I say.
Philemon 1:21 NKJV

Today's Prayer
Dear Lord, being with You can be a wonderful opportunity to make discoveries and enjoy new experiences.
With You by our side, we are safe and well cared for. We ask You to instruct us in the right way to go.
Amen.

Hidden under gardenia leaves at the bush top, a cardinal's nest holds the
treasure of two precious eggs. With building materials delivered by the male,
the female bends them around her body to make a cup.
This process can take three to nine days.[5]

Treasure Five
God Shelters Us

Canada's national bird is a loon,
and the coin bearing that image is nicknamed a loonie.
The date on this one is 1994. The very deep reason
(read an ironic tone here) I picked this one:
it is a bird, similar to the picture of the cardinal nest.

As frail beings, we need shelter. We look for places to call home. Sometimes the structures are elaborate and expensive. In other situations, the buildings are simple. Even twigs, moss, and leaves can be utilized. A cardinal constructs a nest without benefit of hands, using her beak to weave a circular home. If a bird is capable of such complex work, how much more can God do through us?

I long to dwell in your tent forever and take refuge
in the shelter of your wings.
Psalm 61:4

Today's Prayer
Dear Lord, too often we define ourselves by our houses or offices. We stand beside edifices of stone or brick
made by our hands. But these monuments miss the greater security of resting in Your shadow.
Just as the little cardinal creates a home for her young and carefully guards her treasure, please help us
labor with You to make our families secure. Thank You for seeing to our every need.
Amen.

Coins feature portraits of national leaders and icons.
These change over time, and value is not guaranteed.
However, in God's economy, we can—with absolute certainty—count on this: the value of
one life redeemed remains eternal.

Treasure Six
Heavenly Currency
Never Fluctuates

*In the years I have collected coins and shared them with
students as a way of exploring geography and cultures, I realize
how many changes there are in the things various nations deem important.
Figureheads and symbols alter—even materials. The only constant bitcoin is God.*

My coin collection started with a few my father had received from his mother. The hobby continued as I traveled overseas and examined shiny metal for unique pictures and designs. Soon, friends and students shared simple souvenirs from their vacations. Though of no value to collectors, they held sentimental connections for me. During a semester abroad, I discovered Italy's multi-metal artwork. While studying Caribbean literature in Barbados, I saw flying fish splashing across waves, as well as on their money. Each coin reveals a clue about the country's culture. In 1955, President Dwight D. Eisenhower signed into law that US coins and bills must be printed with, "In God We Trust."[6] Cold War angst encouraged citizens to look for Divine help. We would be wise to continue that tradition.

He will be the sure foundation for your times, a rich store of salvation and wisdom

and knowledge; the fear of the LORD is the key to this treasure.

Isaiah 33:6

Today's Prayer
*Dear Lord, whether the stock market is bear or bull, we are certain You provide.
Thank You for Your many generous gifts! Your presence is constant.
Amen.*

This Mono fish is known by its more common name, diamond fish, due to its glittery shape. It prefers brackish water to salt water and does best in schools of five or more. Mono fish reach a size of about six inches and live from seven to ten years.[7] The background is blown-glass artwork displayed in an aquarium.

Treasure Seven
Godly Accounts Paid on Time

*While doing a summer Caribbean literature course
in Barbados, I collected this coin with the flying fish emblem
for the proud island country. Their hospitality was amazing.
Famous poet Kamau Brathwaite wrote, "Each language like a big pot o' Bajan soup …"
in his collection titled* Barabajan Poems.[8] *This was my first time living as a minority,
and the experience proved invaluable in understanding how outsiders feel.*

Managing money is a skill, no matter where we live. Tracking payments and income with a written budget helps us know better how to plan. Even so, unexpected expenses will arise. A medical bill or car repair can put us in a tailspin, wondering how we will cover costs. In those stressful times, we can learn to trust like Peter did in the Bible passage from Matthew 17. When Peter feared how to pay taxes, Jesus told him to go fish.

Jesus said, "But so that we may not cause offense, go to the lake and throw out
your line. Take the first fish you catch; open its mouth and you will find a four-
drachma coin. Take it and give it to them for my tax and yours."
Matthew 17:27

Today's Prayer
*Dear Lord, juggling finances is not my strength. I start well, then fall prey to impulse shopping,
and load up on things I don't need. Please help me have better discipline so my witness is not compromised.
Please connect me with work opportunities where I can labor in faith
to earn what is needed to keep my accounts in good order.
Amen.*

Decorative teacups passed down from my great-grandmother
remind me of the beauty of sharing. Delicate lines on the china and
colorful patterns brighten a day with memories of being loved
and included in special occasions. Though the items don't cost much,
they imprint my heart with pearls of belonging.

Treasure Eight
Fond Memories
Are Prized Heirlooms

*Queen Elizabeth II's seventy-year reign
in the United Kingdom was remarkable. Her sense of tradition and decorum
influenced many. High tea at Harrods is a must when visiting London.
Don't forget the biscuits (cookies). While studying abroad there, my pale complexion
allowed me to blend in ... until I spoke. Surprised at hearing my Southern accent,
the Brits would say, "Blimey, she's a Yank!"*

Family heirlooms are shared through generations, reminding us of special memories. The teacups pictured belonged to my maternal great-grandmother. She loved company and made it an occasion whenever someone visited. She enlisted my help preparing peanut butter and jelly sandwiches for guests. My job was to cut off the brown crust to make perfect white squares. Half a century later, I remember how Nana transformed ordinary ingredients with extraordinary care.

Again, the kingdom of heaven is like a merchant seeking beautiful pearls, who, when
he had found one pearl of great price, went and sold all that he had and bought it.
Matthew 13:45-46 NKJV

Today's Prayer
*Dear Lord, there is nothing more valuable than loved ones. You see us as priceless children and
welcome us into Your heavenly home. We teach young ones their importance by spending quality time with them.
Each occasion shared becomes a polished pearl with eternal significance.
Please inspire us to establish celebrations in everyday circumstances with you.
Amen.*

This jar of pure honey with the honeycomb is hand-poured with love by a family-owned-and-operated apiary. The bees feed on pollen from flowers, such as zinnias, trees, plants, and herbs, near the hives. In the process, the bees serve the vital role of pollinator for farms. The average hive produces more than fifty pounds of surplus honey each year.[9]

Treasure Nine
Kind Words Taste Rich

This petite flower coin is from the Republic of Hungary.
A friend who traveled there for mission work
brought it back for me as a gift.
God "pollinates" hope when his people
spread the good news.

One way to invest in our families and communities is to provide positivity. Kind words encourage and uplift others. When we refrain from complaints and criticisms, we ensure a healthy atmosphere. If something needs to be said, we keep comments concise and focus on how to fix the issue or perform the necessary task. We do not belittle anyone. Pleasant words bring sweetness.

Gracious speech is like clover honey—good taste to the soul,

quick energy for the body.

Proverbs 16:24 MSG

Today's Prayer
Dear Lord, I often speak before thinking. My sharp remarks wound others.
Instead, please help me share gems of praise.
I want to bring a sparkle of joy into the eyes of those who may be underappreciated and weary.
Amen.

This violin has a spruce front and maple back.
The strings should be at a comfortable height for the fingers.
For the instrument to be capable of making good sound,
there must be equal parts quality of materials and care with assembly.

Treasure Ten
Praise Brings God's Presence

This 1988 coin originated in Ireland.
My friend Jody brought it to me.
She loved kissing the Blarney Stone.
The Irish harp has been a national symbol
on coinage since the 1530s.
From folk songs to concertos,
stringed instruments soothe our souls.

Music ushers us into a holy place where our spirit connects with the divine. Listening to instruments has a way of calming the mind and bringing peace. Young David of the Old Testament played a harp to soothe King Saul (1 Samuel 16:23). Conversely, songs can rally us to achieve more. Upbeat tunes energize us. Sports teams often enter the arena to loud, stirring beats. The judge Deborah and Barak, son of Abinoam, sang in celebration after God defeated the enemy for them (Judges 4-5).

The LORD will save me, and we will sing with stringed instruments all the days of
our lives in the temple of the LORD.
Isaiah 38:20

Today's Prayer
Dear Lord, thank You for beautiful melodies and chords that speak to my heart.
Train me to listen for the symphonies of Your love. Help me remember that my joyous praise of You—
particularly in times of difficulty—is a sound that delights Your ears.
Let my voice be in concert with those praising your goodness.
Amen.

An attractive median in downtown Winter Garden, Florida, invites pedestrians to sit on benches under a shady wisteria arbor and listen to the fountain's music. English house sparrows flit back and forth from the branches to sip cool water.

Treasure Eleven
Rebalance Outlook with Faith

The Republic of Hungary chose a falcon
for the forint on this 2001 example.
Falcons must rely on God's provision
for daily survival, just as we do.

Look for opportunities where God provides unexpected resources. The English house sparrow on the facing page found abundant water at a public fountain on a hot summer day. The little creature zoomed up to the pipe and sipped its fill. There was more than enough, but the bird had to be willing to seek. Remaining on a tree branch despairing because there was no nearby lake would have left it parched.

Even the sparrow has found a home,

and the swallow a nest for herself, where she may have her young—

a place near your altar, LORD Almighty,

my King and my God.

Psalm 84:3

Today's Prayer
Dear Lord, I want to be able to move forward in faith.
Please guide me to places where I can find what I need, and give me the strength to fly.
I praise You for the satisfying refreshment provided along the way in this journey of faith.
Amen.

This navel orange is prized for its sweet flavor and juiciness.
The Florida fruit is in season from October through February;
so even in winter, the harvest is plentiful.

Treasure Twelve
No Honor for Fool's Gold

*The crown of Juan Carlos I, king of Spain,
adorns this silver coin.
The image of royalty connects
with the myth of King Midas.
I have never been to Spain;
a former student gave this coin to me.
Sharing stories is a way
to build wisdom and wealth.*

In Greek mythology, King Midas had an opportunity to have a wish granted. Without thinking, he requested that everything he touched turn to gold. Unfortunately, he did not realize the full impact of his choice until he sat at his next meal and could not eat. How often do we crave more, forgetting the abundant blessings at hand?

But these are the ones sown on good ground, those who hear the word, accept it,

and bear fruit: some thirtyfold, some sixty, and some a hundred.

Mark 4:20 NKJV

Today's Prayer
*Dear Lord, please help me see all the gifts I have come to take for granted.
I am blessed with sunshine and rain. Food is available.
I have only to ask you, and my needs are more than met.
When my eyes stray and long for shiny tinsel of no substance, please redirect me to the basics
so I stay grounded in what's important.
Amen.*

In the 1850s, Isaac Singer led a collaboration with several manufacturers to pool patents with Elias Howe's 1846 model. Then they mass-produced a workable sewing machine.[10]

Betsy, my friend from Bible study, made this decorative wall hanging for me.

The artwork brightens my office wall and reminds me that I am important to her.

What creative talent do you have?

Treasure Thirteen
Industry and Imagination Profit

Another example of a royal impression
is the Beatrix Koningin der Nederlanden coin, honoring
the queen of the Netherlands, who reigned from 1980 to 2013.
As a young child, she fled with her family during World War II.
However, she later received permission from both Houses of Parliament
to marry a German diplomat who immediately became a Dutch citizen.[11]
Imagine seamstresses constructing fine garments for her coronation and wedding.

Ordinary fabrics also can serve a godly purpose. A square scrap of fabric from here and there, a bobbin or two, and colorful threads turn into quilted keepsakes. Sewing requires concerted effort, and so does realizing economic advancement. Industry and imagination seam together in the present to craft a beautiful future. With diligence, we can meet needs, as well as generate extra for sharing and comforting others.

In Joppa there was a disciple named Tabitha (in Greek her name is Dorcas); she
was always doing good and helping the poor.

Acts 9:36

Today's Prayer
Dear Lord, Tabitha's friends appreciated the robes and other clothing she made for them.
Her handiwork made them feel special. Her kindness warmed them and restored a sense of dignity.
Please help us labor with dedication and generosity to make our communities better places.
Amen.

This vintage ensemble has rhinestones on the buttons and neckline.
The ruffled cuffs add a nice detail. The blouse was on sale at a downtown thrift store that
accepts donations, and funds care for neglected animals who need shelter.
Everyone benefits from recycling pre-owned clothing.

Treasure Fourteen
Thriftiness Is an Asset

Looking spiffy in his old-fashioned, ruffled collar,
Francisco Hernández de Córdoba (1475–1526)
is considered by some to be the founder of Nicaragua.
He desired physical riches; but God advises us to value
love, joy, peace, patience, kindness, generosity,
faithfulness, gentleness, and self-control.

For an approaching conference, I wanted to look my best. Going to a department store for a new outfit was an option, but I wanted to limit expenditures and pay cash. I popped into a thrift store and rummaged around. Lo and behold, on the back rack, I found the pictured vintage blouse for fifteen dollars. When folks complimented me at the workshop, I smiled and said, "Thank you." I didn't reveal my secret about the attire being a bargain. At the second interview of the day, I got a book contract. This top reminds me that being thrifty won't shortchange good results.

❦

Do not let your adornment be merely outward—arranging the hair,
wearing gold, or putting on fine apparel—rather let it be the hidden person of
the heart, with the incorruptible beauty of a gentle and quiet spirit,
which is very precious in the sight of God.
1 Peter 3:3-4 NKJV

Today's Prayer
Dear Lord, credit cards can be good tools. But exercising discipline to save, then paying with cash,
is wise to avoid temptations to overspend. Please give me a keen eye for bargains
and lead me to shops where I can find what I need for a reasonable cost.
Amen.

Conch and other shells are the currency of the sea. Ever wonder how far one has traveled
or how many times it has rolled in the waves? The mollusks that live inside are delicate,
slimy invertebrates. They take in minerals from the water for food, then excrete calcium
carbonate, which hardens on the outside into a sturdy shell that protects them and expands
as they age.[12] When we conduct all our business affairs with honesty, we will not tumble.

Treasure Fifteen
Integrity Protects the Portfolio

The radiant sun on this coin connects
with the beach scene pictured. A former student from Asia
gave it to me. I admire her tenacity for learning a new culture
in a full-immersion US classroom. I couldn't even grasp her alphabet,
much less survive daily lectures in a second language.
Google Lens identifies the fen as from the Republic of China.

Tides of culture pull at us from many directions. We can be tossed and turned trying to please others. However, if we practice integrity in all we do, God will bless our endeavors. He will reward honesty. If we commit to doing something, we must follow through. If we doubt our ability to deliver, we should refrain from making promises.

And don't say anything you don't mean. … You only make things worse when you
lay down a smokescreen of pious talk, saying, "I'll pray for you," and never doing
it, or saying, "God be with you," and not meaning it. You don't make your words
true by embellishing them with religious lace. … Just say "yes" and "no." When
you manipulate words to get your own way, you go wrong.
Matthew 5:33-37 MSG

Today's Prayer
Dear Lord, please guard my mouth from saying untruths. Even little white lies erode trust.
Please help me build solid relationships based on open communication.
Help me to be known as trustworthy in all that I do.
Amen.

At sunset, a ship cruises in Clearwater Beach, Florida, below one of the city's twenty-six bridges.[13] The first bridge to the island, nicknamed Old Rickety, was built of wood in 1917.[14] This concrete six-lane causeway is quite an advancement.

Each step of faith forward builds more confidence.

Treasure Sixteen
God Bridges Gaps

Stately ancient columns on the coin
resemble those of the modern bridge.
Apaxmai is on one side, designating the country as Greece,
with the structure probably the Parthenon.
Our lives are a monument to God's goodness.
What are you building today to last?

Bridges connect one area to the next over what otherwise might be impossible to traverse. There is a starting point and a definite destination, even if that endpoint may not be in full view. We commit to moving forward. This is what happened to Jacob in Genesis 28. His father sent him away to establish himself in new territory. Near Haran (Turkey),[15] Jacob slept, dreaming of a ladder reaching to Heaven. He saw angels ascending and descending from there to earth. In the vision, God appeared and promised to secure Jacob wherever he went (Genesis 28:10-15).

How awesome is this place!
This is none other than the house of God,
and this is the gate of heaven!
Genesis 28:17 NKJV

Today's Prayer
Dear Lord, I often make the mistake of wanting change but am unwilling to do anything differently.
Please show me the direction to take to see new ventures that will grow my faith and strengthen my character.
Help me leave behind old habits that hold me back.
Amen.

This snowy egret perches by the dock, anticipating abundance in the harbor where many charter boats launch. Snacks are sure to abound soon.

Treasure Seventeen
Anticipate Abundance

This Portuguese coin features a ship powered by the wind.
"The wind blows wherever it pleases. You hear its sound,
but you cannot tell where it comes from or where it is going.
So it is with everyone born of the Spirit" (John 3:8).
God moves in ways we can't always see or predict,
but His direction is apparent when hearts
sail toward truth.

Sometimes the wallet empties before we're ready. The bank account dips, and we grow fearful regarding how to make ends meet. When we hit these times of wondering how everything will work out, we can recall what happened when Peter and several disciples went fishing (John 21:1-14). They were out all night but caught nothing. Discouraged and weary, they came ashore the next morning empty-handed. Jesus saw them and asked if they had any food. When they answered no, He told them where to fish. Then they caught so much they almost capsized the boat.

Simon Peter went up and dragged the net to land, full of large fish, one hundred
and fifty-three; and although there were so many, the net was not broken.
John 21:11 NKJV

Today's Prayer
Dear Lord, in the times when expenses threaten to exceed income,
please help me position in faith and wait for Your guidance on how to proceed.
I watch for Your deliverance. Thank You for the abundance about to occur.
Amen.

Hospitality invites others to enjoy blessings we've received.

A basket of cranberry muffins with a pecan braid makes a nice gift for neighbors.

When we welcome people into our homes, we have an opportunity to deepen relationships.

Cheerful sharing multiplies the impact of God's gifts.

Treasure Eighteen
Givers Gain, Not Lose

*A French woman sows seeds with the sun
rising in the background. Without plantings,
there would be no harvest for making breads. Bakers rise early
to invest effort to create tasty croissants with chocolate filling.
These treats captivated me while visiting Paris.*

The pleasing aroma of baking bread and cinnamon fills a kitchen and draws family members toward the table. God has wonderful things to serve. He delights in setting the table with delicious food. He distributes resources in such a way to encourage us to share. One may have butter, while another has extra flour. Someone else has sugar and pecans. A recipe for satisfaction comes with generosity. By combining our ingredients, we create a feast for all.

If you come with us, we will share with you
whatever good things the LORD gives us.
Numbers 10:32

Today's Prayer
*Dear Lord, too often I clutch what is in my hand because I fear shortage.
Yet Your storehouse is overflowing, and it pleases You to see me share.
As I demonstrate generosity, You bless me with more because You know good will result.
Please show me how to be a cheerful giver.
Amen.*

Seeking a heavenly perspective requires lifting our eyes.

When we pause and survey matters with God's help and insights,

we understand better how choices impact the future.

We can pray and position for long-term benefits, without regrets.

Treasure Nineteen
Look for Long-Term Investments

*Pegasus was the Greek mythological steed
that carried Zeus's thunder and lightning but knew not
to approach Olympus uninvited. I wonder at the freedom
to take flight and soar. The first time I ever flew as a child,
I looked for angels sitting in the clouds.*

At street level, we see a block or so in front of us. However, with an aerial perspective, we can study miles ahead and map the best routes. This ability to gauge actions based on future needs also works for finances. If we tie up all our assets circling the cul-de-sac of immediate gratification, we run out of fuel to travel long distances. With a plan and a written budget, we can navigate with confidence to a secure destination.

Trust God from the bottom of your heart;
don't try to figure out everything on your own.
Listen for God's voice in everything you do, everywhere you go;
he's the one who will keep you on track.
Proverbs 3:5-6 MSG

Today's Prayer
*Dear Lord, I like to buy things now, but lack of forethought can cause difficulties down the road.
Please guide me to advisors and planning resources to help me map out wise investments that will grow over time.
Please help me avoid the temptation of frivolous purchases that don't build my portfolio.
Amen.*

Bits of colored glass and dangly settings make for a colorful jewelry display.

Each piece could be a prayer offered up to Jesus to hold dear.

These adorn His holy tunic as He enters the throne room to intercede on our behalf.

The watch reminds us that prayers transcend time; they are stored in Heaven.

(See Revelation 5:8 and 8:3–4)

Treasure Twenty
Gems of Prayer Adorn Christ

Venus, the long-haired beauty
on this euro coin from Italy,
is modeled after the work
by the famous artist Sandro Botticelli.
God can inspire artwork
to reveal His intricacy.

In ancient Jewish tradition, the high priest wore sacred clothing—consisting of a tunic, or *ephod*, with a jewel-adorned breastplate—whenever he entered the holy place (Exodus 28). When I think of Jesus as our Intercessor today, I imagine Him wearing a holy garment with our prayers sparkling on His vest of righteousness. He bears our names over His heart as a continuing memorial before the Lord. Each sincere petition we raise in His name shines forth the radiance of hope.

Then mount four rows of precious stones on it. The first row shall be carnelian,
chrysolite and beryl; the second row shall be turquoise, lapis lazuli and emerald;
the third row shall be jacinth, agate and amethyst; the fourth row shall be topaz,
onyx and jasper. Mount them in gold filigree settings.
Exodus 28:17-20

Today's Prayer
Dear Lord, whenever I see or wear jewelry, let the beautiful objects remind me how precious
I am to You and that Jesus keeps my prayers on His heart like holy gems.
Amen.

Wall decor in a French pastry shop resembles an old-fashioned oven.
The brick pattern radiates outward, as should our praise of what God
accomplishes. Whether or not we give Him credit when success comes our way
is a measure of our spiritual maturity. When we receive a compliment,
do we puff up or acknowledge God's help?

Treasure Twenty-One
Give God Credit

Brazil's Emperor Pedro I rides to proclaim independence.
While we want to stand up for Christian principles,
we don't want to trample others in the process.
"A gentle answer turns away wrath,
but a harsh word stirs up anger"
(Proverbs 15:1).

During adversity, we often cry out to God for relief. These times test our faith and distill our beliefs about what we can rely upon. While we try to avoid trials, what if God intends them to bring good? Silver is refined with high heat that melts away impurities. To achieve the greatest value, gold ore also must be cleansed of minerals, such as copper, aluminum, and iron. Gold must be heated to an excess of 2,150 degrees Fahrenheit to be purified.[16] One test we must withstand is becoming prideful. We need to acknowledge God's input in every achievement.

The crucible for silver and the furnace for gold,
but people are tested by their praise.
Proverbs 27:21

Today's Prayer
Dear Lord, King Solomon advised his sons in Proverbs not to let accolades from others taint a person's self-perception.
Any achievements we accomplish are empowered by You. Thank You for victories.
We know nothing is possible without Your favor and equipping.
Amen.

Guard wisdom as a precious treasure year-round.
Attractive decorations delight the eye,
and sound advice secures purchasing decisions
in all seasons.

Treasure Twenty-Two
Wisdom before Rubies

*My son traveled to Egypt and brought back this coin
with the image of a sphinx. I think about how the tombs
were to be sacred, but robbers pillaged them.
God would have us store up treasures of the heart.
We can't take gold or silver with us
when it is our time to go.*

Training our eyes to see lasting value takes practice. There are many worldly distractions that look lovely, but their exteriors may crack or chip over time. What we want in the moment may soon cause disenchantment if we aren't careful. Only God's truths will keep us grounded. Good judgment develops as we follow the Bible's teachings, and we gain insights on how to manage money. Wisdom is the ability to apply God's guidance in everyday decisions.

Receive my instruction, and not silver, and knowledge rather than choice gold;
for wisdom is better than rubies, and all the things one may desire
cannot be compared with her.
Proverbs 8:10-11 NKJV

Today's Prayer
*Dear Lord, please give me a desire to read the Bible and the ability to understand the teachings.
Like the wise men who followed the star, I want to find Jesus.
Amen.*

A silk sponge from Tarpon Springs, Florida, and fragrant soaps make bath time pleasant and refreshing. Soaking in a hot, bubble-filled tub washes away the day's irritations and shortcomings. At night, ask God to put a new spirit in you so you can begin the next day with a clear conscience and a balanced outlook.

Treasure Twenty-Three
Keep Transactions Clean

The Hong Kong orchid tree blooms with a five-petaled flower.
Natural ingredients come from flowers
and often perfume specialty soaps.
As we conduct our daily business,
do we leave behind a fragrance or a stench?

Housekeeping isn't my favorite chore. If you visit my home, things appear tidy on the surface, but whatever you do, don't look too closely. I have to work at the deep cleaning to keep my residence spotless. Exercising discipline on a daily basis to polish my heart's outlook also is needed to keep my attitude maintained well.

I will sprinkle clean water on you, and you will be clean;

I will cleanse you from all your impurities and from all your idols.

I will give you a new heart and put a new spirit in you;

I will remove from you your heart of stone and give you a heart of flesh.

And I will put my Spirit in you and move you to follow

my decrees and be careful to keep my laws.

Ezekiel 36:25-27

Today's Prayer
Dear Lord, there are icky parts to my life I tend to ignore. Things may look okay on the surface;
but there are underlying issues that need to be addressed so sin doesn't creep in and consume me.
Please shower me with Your love so I have the will and commitment to do what's right.
Amen.

Leather baby shoes were treasured in a tiny cardboard jewelry box

for more than sixty-five years by adoring parents

long after their son reached manhood. As spiritual children,

we crawl and then take our tentative first steps with faith. God is with us.

He cherishes us and holds our hands steady as we venture out.

Treasure Twenty-Four
Stride toward Success

I have no idea how I got this coin.
Google Lens identifies it as a Japanese five-yen.
The round shape denotes the idea of the circle of life.
What legacy are we leaving our descendants,
many of whom we may never meet?
If they follow in our footsteps,
have we guided them to godly territory?

It takes courage to make your dreams a reality. The temptation is to play life safe, hunker down in familiar routines, and bemoan lost opportunities. However, God invites us to step out and adventure toward the land of milk and honey. There will be times of wilderness as we journey, but they refine us to become better stewards of the abundance He has waiting. As we move forward to claim new territory for God's people, the inheritance for future generation expands.

The LORD makes firm the steps of the one who delights in him; though he may
stumble, he will not fall, for the LORD upholds him with his hand.
Psalm 37:23-24

Today's Prayer
Dear Lord, when dissatisfaction creeps in and nothing seems to satisfy, please help me determine if that is greed
or Your sovereign call to go further than I believed possible. Please give me courage to venture out,
believing in faith that I can do more for Your kingdom to better the lives of those around me.
Amen.

Summer is the season to bale hay. The timing must be right for rain to nourish grass seeds, yet there also must be sunny days for the cuttings to dry. Without labor in the hot months, there will not be sufficient food for livestock in the winter.

How far-reaching is your financial plan?

Treasure Twenty-Five
Blessings Flow to the Faithful

Mythology credits Minerva (Greeks called her Athena)
for giving an olive tree to foster wisdom and peace.
The Italian coin commemorates this.
Agriculture requires steadfastness to render a crop.
If we seek knowledge from the Bible,
we can be assured of the right harvest.

Farmers plant tiny seeds, then water and fertilize them. They wait days, months, and sometimes years for crops to mature. Workers of the land husband resources to ensure safety against inclement weather and invading insects. Farmers don't give up. They know they need to provide nourishing food for people and animals. How often do we nurture our faith by feeding on the good words in the Bible? Without God's Word as our staple, we cannot sustain our efforts and reap a healthy crop.

The Lord will send a blessing on your barns and on everything you put your hand
to. The Lord your God will bless you in the land he is giving you. The Lord
will establish you as his holy people, as he promised you on oath, if you keep the
commands of the Lord your God and walk in obedience to him.
Deuteronomy 28:8-9

Today's Prayer
Dear Lord, quite frankly, I grow tired of working. Days seem long, and returns often seem slight.
Please help me see the possibilities ahead so I don't give up when the crop is still growing and in need of tending.
Amen.

Storms are inevitable. When they loom on the horizon, what do we do?
Rather than give in to fear, we can petition God for His protection.
He hears us and will move on our behalf to provide shelter.

Treasure Twenty-Six
Only God Ensures Security

*Minted in 1976, this atomic coin from Greece signified the
contribution of Greek philosopher Democritus (460 to 370 BC)
to the atomic theory of the universe. Centuries later,
we are still grasping how to understand God's complex design.
I connect the idea of the water cycle with electrons
zig-zagging around in a thunderstorm.*

Lightning flashes across the sky. Monstrous bully clouds saunter closer, flexing muscles and wearing evil grins. There is no escape. The only hope is to find refuge. After we run inside for protection, the view changes. What seemed threatening before transforms into a fantastical firework show under God's complete control. He is mighty. With Him as our champion, there is nothing to fear.

Lord, you have been our dwelling place throughout all generations.
Before the mountains were born or you brought forth the whole world,
from everlasting to everlasting you are God.
Psalm 90:1-2

Today's Prayer
*Dear Lord, please teach us to number our days so that we gain a heart of wisdom.
We are grateful for Your protection and shelter.
When terror tries to overtake us, please draw us into Your loving embrace.
Amen.*

Strawberries are in the top-three category for favorite fruit for Americans. California alone
is reported to produce so many strawberries in one year that if they were laid berry to berry,
they would circle the earth fifteen times.[17]

How sweet are words of fellowship and encouragement.

Imagine their effect enriching others with love.

Treasure Twenty-Seven
Harvest Good Will

A cornucopia of harvest decorates this 1996 coin from Peru.
I like the little llama in the background too.
The coin also depicts a cinchona tree, with leaves that provided
chemicals for the world's first anti-malarial drug.
God's Word to us also is healing.

In a world full of criticism and judgment, how delicious are kind words that soothe arguments and heal broken hearts. The Bible teaches us to love one another, which is not an easy assignment. We get on each other's nerves and fail to deliver on promises. However, God is faithful and teaches us how to be kind. His largesse endows us with the ability to show grace to others.

But the seed in the good earth—these are the good-hearts who seize the Word and

hold on no matter what, sticking with it until there's a harvest.

Luke 8:15 MSG

Today's Prayer
Dear Lord, I want the fruit of my life to be fragrant and wholesome.
In places where there is blight, please heal. Please protect the crop of my actions from pests that would destroy.
Help my countenance shine with Your love to draw others near.
Amen.

A massive crane aligns a concrete wall for a new school, while a road grader smooths the pathway for the street. Workers coordinate efforts to meet deadlines and ensure safety. In the same way, God constructs teams to achieve the purposes He has set out for building a holy kingdom.
Establishing walls of righteousness protect all.

Treasure Twenty-Eight
Leverage God's Might

*The Morgan Lewis windmill
is on a twenty-five-cent piece from Barbados
and represents the history of sugar cane.
When we offer kind words,
we build up others.*

Many tasks look monumental until we invite God onto the job site. He will add His strength and resources to equip us to do what otherwise would be impossible. The foundation is poured believing His purposes are good and true. Upon that solid understanding, we can construct secure walls of life experiences where we see His hand at work. We are not alone in any endeavor.

Unless the LORD builds the house, the builders labor in vain. Unless the LORD
watches over the city, the guards stand watch in vain.

Psalm 127:1

Today's Prayer
*Dear Lord, sometimes my life looks like a disaster zone.
Debris is everywhere; I don't know how to put things together.
Please superintend assembly so that a strong structure results that will shelter many and bring You glory.
Amen.*

For half a century, I have saved family correspondence and love letters, notes of consolation
and encouragement, and well wishes for anniversaries and birthdays.
All of these represent moments of deep caring recorded for safekeeping.
The Bible is God's sacred collection of love letters to us.

Treasure Twenty-Nine
Save Letters of Love

Jesus is referred to as the lion (Revelation 5:5)
and the lamb (John 1:29).
The image on this ten-pence British coin of the lion
wearing a crown makes me smile.

Letters and cards sent by friends and family are saved in a special place in my house. They date back half a century and include childhood birthday cards from my grandparents, who have long since left this earth. There are love letters and notes of encouragement, even a homecoming date invitation from high school. Simple drawings from children and former students document affection. The Bible is God's correspondence to His family, recording His love, cautions for safety, and constancy.

When the kindness and love of God our Savior appeared, he saved us, not because
of righteous things we had done, but because of his mercy.
Titus 3:4-5

Today's Prayer
Dear Lord, words are powerful, particularly written ones.
These messages survive, often long after the scribe, to secure future generations.
Thank You for the centuries of love You pour out and the love letters You pen in the Bible.
Please inspire me today to write a note telling a person how important he or she is and how much he or she is loved.
Amen.

Ancient mariners navigated by constellations at night.

They deciphered movement of the heavenly bodies to align their course and not get lost.

Though we may pride ourselves today on satellites and global positioning devices,

the only infallible way to journey is with God beside us.

Treasure Thirty
God Is the Treasure We Seek

*This 1999 Kuwaiti coin with an Arab sailing vessel
is the third coin my son gave me.
On life's journey, are we trusting God
to guide us forward into new adventures?*

God is right now. Although the Bible assembles His ancient stories that were collected across centuries, the Word also unveils prophecies to be fulfilled in times to come. But the most startling gift is that God is present with us. With Him, we can overcome every obstacle and enjoy a life well lived.

Let them praise the name of the Lord, for his name alone is exalted; his splendor
is above the earth and the heavens.

Psalm 148:13

Today's Prayer
*Dear Lord, explorers of old set sail to find riches untold.
They risked everything to pursue dreams beyond the mysterious horizon.
We believe in You and Your goodness. We know You love us.
Thank You for wise counsel to ensure we invest our lives with purpose
and share the priceless treasures of faith and hope.
Amen.*

Acknowledgments

Gratitude goes to Ambassador International and the team for believing in the devotional's message and championing production. Early contributors to conceptual design include Mari Gonzales, Kathy Ide, and Jonathan Lewis.

Musician Pete Bonaskiewich offered terrific hospitality and a beautiful impromptu concert.

My friend Betsy Johnson makes beautiful quilts and welcomed me into her sewing room.

Kenny Lambourdiere organized a fantastic trip to Clearwater Beach. The sunset cruise was beautiful, and the surprise cake shared by the generous wedding party was very sweet.

Kaley Rhea offered invaluable insights how to improve the manuscript with her tender heart and vast editorial knowledge.

Jackie Howe is a terrific friend, always available to take road trips as well as to offer counseling when I have a panic attack. Thank you for your support through lots of drama.

Rosallie in Winter Garden, Florida, serves delicious Quiche Lorraine in a handsome European café.

Blue Letter Bible is a terrific research tool for studying and locating Bible passages in many versions. https://www.blueletterbible.org.

Thanks to all who bring beauty in ordinary circumstances and invest in kindness. You make this world a wonderful place!

Persis Abraham of Art Innovations (www.artinnovations.in) designed a gorgeous interior layout with meticulous detail.

Deb, Craig, Stephen, Madalyn, Paisley, and Leah helped with puppy ops. What a hoot playing chase!

(Author's Note: Facts about the coins are not exhaustive. Only my recollection and observations are recorded. As the coins were collected during several decades, my memory of who provided what is incomplete. If you have specific details to add about any of the coins or their history, please correspond through my website at www.tracysmoak.com.)

Endnotes

This small coin commemorates the bravery of one of Panama's indigenous chiefs, Urraca. He battled Spanish conquistadors in the sixteenth century.[18] However, the country's national currency is named the Panamanian balboa after the Spanish explorer Vasco Nunez de Balboa who founded the first European settlement there.[19]

1   Zachary Crockett, "How Rich Would You Be if You Actually Got a Penny for Every Thought," December 6, 2016, https://www.vox.com/culture/2016/12/6/13821430/penny-every-thought-rich.

2   "King James Bible, 1611," British Library, July 17, 2022 at https://www.bl.uk/collection-items/king-james-bible#.

3   Donald W. Hall, "Eastern Black Swallowtail," Entomology and Nematology Department, University of Florida, March 2021, https://entnemdept.ufl.edu/creatures/bfly/bfly2/eastern_black_swallowtail.htm.

4   Dictionary.com "Eire," April 13, 2023, https://www.dictionary.com/browse/eire#:~:text=definitions%20for%20Eire-,Eire,Irish%20Gaelic%20name%20for%20Ireland.

5   Jason Martin and Robyn Bailey, "Why So, Mr. Cardinal? NestWatch Explains," The Cornell Lab, March 5, 2013, https://www.allaboutbirds.org/news/why-so-red-mr-cardinal-nestwatch-explains.

6   "The Legislation Placing 'In God We Trust' on National Currency," US House of Representatives: History, Art & Archives, https://history.house.gov/HistoricalHighlight/Detail/36275.

7   "Mono Fish," Animal-World Pet and Animal Information, July 10, 2022, https://animal-world.com/mono-argentus-fingerfish.

8   Kamau Brathwaite, *Barabajan Poems*, (Jamaica: Savacou Publications, 1994) 49.

9   "How Honey Is Made," National Honey Board, Accessed July 18, 2022, https://honey.com/about-honey/how-honey-is-made#.

10 Jimmy Stamp, "The Many, Many Designs of the Sewing Machine," *Smithsonian Magazine*, October 16, 2013, https://www.smithsonianmag.com/arts-culture/the-many-many-designs-of-the-sewing-machine-2142740/#.

11 Royal House of the Netherlands, Princess Beatrix, Marriage and Family, https://www.royal-house.nl/members-royal-house/princess-beatrix/marriage-and-family.

12 "Wonder of the Day #1250: How Are Sea Shells Formed," National Center for Families Learning, https://www.wonderopolis.org/wonder/how-are-sea-shells-formed#.

13 Chris George, "Clearwater to make repairs to 14 bridges," *Tampa Bay Newspapers*, October 29, 2021, https://www.tbnweekly.com/clearwater_beacon/article_04c42c6c-3684-11ec-b94c-23daba74fa5c.html.

14 Gabrielle Calise, "How has Clearwater Beach evolved over the past century? Florida Wonders explores," *Tampa Bay Times*, May 2, 2019, https://www.tampabay.com/florida/2019/05/02/how-has-clearwater-beach-evolved-over-the-past-century-florida-wonders-investigates.

15 *Britannica*, s.v. "Harran," April 3, 2020, https://www.britannica.com/place/Harran.

16 "Gold Commodity Chain," The Ohio State University, July 30, 2022, https://u.osu.edu/goldcommoditychain/smelting/#.

17 David Trinklein, "Strawberry: A Brief History," Curators of the University of Missouri, May 21, 2012, https://ipm.missouri.edu/meg/2012/5/Strawberry-A-Brief-History.

18 "The Territories of Urraca," Anywhere Panama, Accessed April 14, 2023 https://www.anywhere.com/panama/destinations/chitre/tours/territories-urraca.

19 James Chen, "Panamanian Balboa (PAB): Meaning, History, Economy of Panama," Investopedia, August 17, 2022, https://www.investopedia.com/terms/forex/p/pab-panama-balboa.asp.

About the Author

A native Floridian, Tracy L. Smoak grew up in Clermont riding horses and climbing citrus trees. Her passion is to encourage others in their faith journey. Smoak contributes to Guideposts. In addition to her debut novel with Ambassador International, *Who Brought the Dog to Church?*, Bold Vision publishes her Bible study about encouragement *Refuge of Grace: Finding Your Safe Place*.

She loves photography and authored two other hardcover devotionals with her original pictures *Living Water to Refresh Your Soul* and *Arranged with Love*.

Smoak holds a master's in education and a bachelor's in communication. At her church home, she leads small-group Bible studies. She is an active member of Word Weavers International.

You can find Tracy at
www.tracysmoak.com
Devotions with her photography set to music are available on YouTube at
www.youtube.com/@tracysmoak/playlists.

Ambassador International's mission is to magnify the Lord Jesus Christ and promote His Gospel through the written word.

We believe through the publication of Christian literature, Jesus Christ and His Word will be exalted, believers will be strengthened in their walk with Him, and the lost will be directed to Jesus Christ as the only way of salvation.

For more information about
AMBASSADOR INTERNATIONAL
please visit:

www.ambassador-international.com
www.facebook.com/AmbassadorIntl

@AmbassadorIntl

Thank you for reading this book.
Please consider leaving us a review on your social media, favorite retailer's website, Goodreads, Bookbub, or our website.